Also by Marc Kaminsky

Poetry

A Cleft in the Rock (2018)
Shadow Traffic (2008)
Target Populations (1991)
The Road from Hiroshima (1984)
Daily Bread (1984)
A Table with People (1982)
A New House (1974)
Birthday Poems (1972)

Prose

What's Inside You It Shines Out of You (1974)

Editor

Stories as Equipment for Living: Last Talks and Tales of Barbara Myerhoff. Co-edited with Mark Weiss in collaboration with Deena Metzger (2007)
Remembered Lives: The Work of Ritual, Storytelling and Growing Older, by Barbara Myerhoff (1992)
The Uses of Reminiscence (1984)
The Book of Autobiographies (1982)
The Journal Project: Pages from the Lives of Old People (1980)

Theater Pieces

In the Traffic of a Targeted City (1986)
Worksong (in collaboration with the Talking Band, 1978)

The Stones
of Lifta

Marc Kaminsky

DOS MADRES
2019

DOS MADRES PRESS INC.
P.O.Box 294, Loveland, Ohio 45140
www.dosmadres.com   editor@dosmadres.com

Dos Madres is dedicated to the belief that the small press is essential to the vitality of contemporary literature as a carrier of the new voice, as well as the older, sometimes forgotten voices of the past. And in an ever more virtual world, to the creation of fine books pleasing to the eye and hand.

Dos Madres is named in honor of Vera Murphy and Libbie Hughes, the "Dos Madres" whose contributions have made this press possible.

Dos Madres Press, Inc. is an Ohio Not For Profit Corporation and a 501 (c) (3) qualified public charity. Contributions are tax deductible.

Executive Editor: Robert J. Murphy

Illustration & Book Design: Elizabeth H. Murphy
www.illusionstudios.net

Typeset in Adobe Garamond Pro & Trajan Pro
ISBN 978-1-948017-58-9
Library of Congress Control Number: 2019945605

First Edition
Copyright 2019 Marc Kaminsky
All rights reserved. No part of this book may be reproduced or transmitted in any form or by any means graphic, electronic or mechanical, including photocopying, recording, taping or by any information storage or retrieval system, without the permission in writing from the publisher.
Published by Dos Madres Press, Inc.

TO MENACHEM DAUM

TABLE OF CONTENTS

I. The Impasse

Hinani 1
Impasse 2
In Jerusalem Stone 4
The Domes of Lifta 7
The Return 11
Lifta Fugue 12

II. Front Lines

Birth Trauma 17
Gray Bird 19
Constellations of Lifta 21
On the Front Lines 22
After His Likeness 23
The World to Come 25

III. On the Site of Loss

The Coffee House at Lifta 29
The Gift 34
In Bethlehem 39
None to Accompany Me 40
The Key 42
Going Home 46

IV. On the Road to Jerusalem

At the Missing Hearth 51
First Cousins 53
Remorse 62
The Messiah 65
Visitation 68
Disbelief 70
Next Year in Jerusalem 71

Acknowledgments 75
A Note about the Author 77

I.
The Impasse

Hinani

Unworthy as I am, when I saw
footage of my friend Menachem climbing beneath
the Jerusalem hills with an old man—
a displaced person—an Arab
who guided him into the ruins of his home
in Lifta, I felt something
become as clear and actual to me
as if for one pulse beat I heard
a voice speaking to my heart.

Call it the divine, it is the voice that calls
to us once or twice in a lifetime.
We recognize it immediately and answer, Here I am,
for we remember it from before
we were born, and remain ready all our lives to go
where it sends us. It spoke clearly
and distinctly as I sat with Menachem
in my Brooklyn office, watching
his unfinished film, it said to me, Go
to Lifta, accompany your friend to the emptied village
of Lifta, walk beside him as he treads carefully
around the boulder that blocks the winding path up to Lifta.

IMPASSE

Yacoub Odeh, a spokesman for the stones
of Lifta, calls the remains of his village an eyewitness
to history. For Itzik Shweky, spokesman
of the Society for the Preservation of Heritage Sites,
it's an eyesore at the western gate of Jerusalem.
Israelis would rather not be reminded of what happened
here every time they drive in and out of the city.

Yacoub takes foreign journalists to the wadi,
now a mikvah, around which his ancestors built
their homes in this bowl of fertile land.
He stands at the top of the hillside and calls,
Uncle! to show how he lived as a boy
within earshot of his whole world. He slogs
through waist-high weeds, cacti, untended
fig trees to an archway that now opens onto air,
points to a relief carved in the stone,
a pattern that repeats the promise of return,
and reads the Arabic inscription, Enter safely.

Ours is the last Palestinian village in Israel
that hasn't been torn down or resettled.
They want to turn our houses into 54 villas
and build 158 luxury condos, a mall,
a synagogue, a five-star hotel and a museum
for artifacts from Lifta. My memories
of home, mosque, spring water, cemetery
will never fit into their museum. Why
can't I return to my village?

And Itzik Shweky answers: If I let Lifta stand
as a monument that says on this site
there was an Arab village, it would lead
to painful memories and hatred, I
would be causing conflict. They will say,
"This is how we once lived and then
the Jews came and threw us out." No!
I'm not going to let that happen.

And Yacoub Odeh answers: This
is how we once lived and then
the Jews came and kicked us out. I
left my village 64 years ago, but surely
I will come back again, and if not
I, then my children.

In Jerusalem Stone

Stone of our fathers, stone
that we gather in the house-to-
house war for Eretz Yisrael,
the white Jerusalem stone

of which Lifta was built
unveils the village of strangers
as our own place of hospitality,
every last stone!

for the Above is foundation
of the below, so it is
that each stone must bear the weight
of the land beneath it.

•

For the power of stone lies
in its mute testimony, it speaks
to us as the final settlement
of fact, so that we never forget

the living secret it contains—
malleable as flesh
in our hands, when it yields,
it spouts the water of life.

•

And every shard
bequeathed to us at Sinai
is an eternal deed,
so archeology turns

into a handmaiden of real
estate developers, and city
officials are equipped with
the rod of Moses, we read

the hand of God in stone
worked by our ancestors
and write new certificates
of occupancy in old stone.

•

Blown for centuries from
one place to another,
we treasure stone
of the hearth above all

things, but the ruins
of our enemy's home
present a danger
to the history of divine

right and exclusive possession
that we find in Jerusalem
stone, for he claims that
from his ancestral stones

memories also run like
water, and he hurls them
against us, so it is
that we must dismantle

his house stone
by stone, and haul
it away
to build the oblivion

of his past
and the absence
of a future for him
behind our territorial wall.

The Domes of Lifta

Tonight, walking away the hills
that separate me
from my village, I behold
my home, veiled
in the light of a crescent moon:

it's a face with two
blind eyes and a toothless
mouth, yet it knows I am
there—why else
would it stare at me
with so fixed a gaze?

And I see Lifta passing
the hours of widowhood
praying that I come
out of her dream
that I am dreaming of her
and enter her in the flesh.

•

Each home in Lifta was like
the other: a great cube
topped by a dome. The eye
naturally completed the circle
inside the square: eternity
finding shelter on earth.

•

Lifta is now a black dot on the Corpus
Separatum. Who remembers this
was the name given to the Green Line
that marked the place where the two
armies stopped fighting? It was erased

years ago from Israeli maps, but
Lifta remains as a sign of the body
of land separating bloodshed
and negotiation, the demilitarized zone,
the border until the warring parties

make peace. Now the occupier wants
to bury Lifta along with the armistice
line. To him, it's a corpse, rotting
in the valley below his city. To me,
its yellow stone revives the smell
of my early years. The musk of home
wasn't dispersed when they drove us out.
They blasted holes in our high-vaulted
ceilings to deny us shelter. We live here
in reverie, resurrecting the domes of Lifta.

•

Our grandfathers quarried the white
and yellow Jerusalem stone and built
our homes with their own hands,
a rare thing in an urban setting.

We joined the communal life
of the town with the rural life
of farmers: our mosque and social
club and coffee houses and schools
for both girls and boys were sustained
by over 4000 dunams of arable land.

Olives and grains in abundance,
the markets of Jerusalem close by,
harmony between neighbors, and
between ourselves and the land,
harmony, each home embedded
in the slope of the hillside, stone
of its stone, no house rose
to block the view of the other.

•

Anyone with eyes that can read
a people in its architecture
can feel what these buildings contained:
eternity was at home in the hours
of our daily round. If I die
without living again in Lifta, if
Lifta and its cemetery are buried
under the Arab-style facades
of a colonial resort, the place
where I was born will go on
being reborn in you,
my children and grandchildren.
You have never seen our village;

nevertheless, when anyone
asks, Where are you from?
you answer, Lifta.

THE RETURN

After and after and after that—
the clock is in the hands of the occupier,
his hours strike me,
they keep me from taking care of my real affairs.
Every day throws me farther away
from my village, but I wait
for the night faithfully to
lift me and carry me into
the midst of before.

At home, my father drinks coffee
from his cup of minutes, my mother's voice
reaches eternity which is lodged on the hillside
where her mother grows
ancestral, my brother and I know that every road
leading out of the village returns.
The spring at the heart of our valley flows
day by day, I touch the dove's wings,
I play flute-songs in the olive grove.

Lifta Fugue

That blur of motion and color flitting
in and out of view as you approach
Jerusalem—that's Lifta. Ruins

that squat on our hillsides,
defacing our land. No one
in his right mind would go there.

Drug dealers and whores lure
lost souls and foreign travelers down
to that desperate spot

on unmarked paths, overhung
by vines and weeds higher than
any man, a black canopy eclipses

the moon and deranges the stars;
you can't get your bearings;
every leaf shivering in the wind

is a ghastly thought; a hand
bursting out of a fig tree
seizes you by the throat,

another dispossesses you
of your shekels, or worse.
A wilderness in our midst,

a spectral village, mired
in bad blood, a breeding ground
of violence, disease and death—

we will restore its Biblical name
and lift it up as a neighbor-
hood thriving in Zion. Already

we have fenced-off the blast-zone,
begun dynamiting through rock,
brought in earth-moving machines

and dump trucks. Soon
an underground tunnel will run
from the Knesset to Mei Niftoach

and we will commute from the City
to a green and luxurious site of
suburban peace in twenty minutes.

II.
FRONT
LINES

II.
FRONT
LINES

Birth Trauma

We were thrown together in the womb of one mother.
My hands curled around his heels, his head dreaming
of the life-to-come lay against a pillow that in time
would become the bony hollow between my breasts,
and we could still speak, specks of two people
floating in the same sea, we could still remember
our previous life, we were partners studying
the sky. I wanted us to continue learning the text
on rain, he demanded that we develop
plans for an irrigation system
that would extend the patrimony of Abraham
onto barren land and multiply its yield.

As my potential hand put out fingers, he felt
sinews bind bone to bone in the hand he pressed
against me, I felt my legs grow long
and flex and expand as we began moving
against each other, he discovered he was gigantic
when suddenly I was all over him, wherever I
turned, there he was, he had me surrounded,
I wrapped my umbilical cord around his neck
and tightened the noose, he slipped through
as he turned into the absence of my lebensraum.

We forgot we were brothers. As the time
for my birth drew near, I pulled his feet
toward the gate of fire so he'd be in no
position to enter, he attacked my head
and pushed it out to the west. No common
memories or speech blunted our fury.

Blind and in danger of being annihilated
by the terrible velocity of the other's weight gain,
we whirled around inside each other's formation
until I was not I apart from the he that is he.

And he grew up inside me as my enemy.
And I am besieged in the bad
dream that's destroyed my peace
from the time before I was born.

Gray Bird

Once, crossing the bridge at Ismalia on my way to Sahar Tumaizi's sweet shop, I passed a gray bird on the ground. Something about it stopped me. It wasn't on its legs, it lay there as if nesting on stone. It took me a while to realize it would never fly again. I sat down next to it. Maybe, if I waited, it would stand up and start pecking. The shouts of the marketplace faded, the cries of the street vendors died out. The bird didn't seem scared, it didn't struggle, it barely looked around. After a time, I stopped feeling my legs underneath me. The bird didn't seem to know I was there. Everything was quiet, except when someone bent over me and brought his or her face close to mine. They wanted to know if I was OK, was the bird my bird, shouldn't I be getting home? It sounded like they were shouting to me from a great distance. These things happen, the bird is just resting, you can't save every pigeon that falls from the sky, you're in the way here, it's sad, but what can you do? They each said something to get me going, and went away.

It got dark. I started to feel my mother's pacing in the kitchen. I could feel her going out of the house and calling to the citrus grove, the barley field, the mountain, the sky. I tried to stand, but my legs were shaking. I tried to walk, the ground plunged needles into my feet. When I reached home, my father beat me. For the next month, I wasn't allowed out on my own. That month the bridge was blown up. I stole out to see it, and found the marketplace gone. Across the ravine, every house was empty. My father joined the Lehi militia and came back with a missing right hand. I lied about my age, they turned a blind eye because I'm Noson Lipovetsky's Benjamin, they took me into his unit. Sometimes, on my way to sleep, I'm crossing the bridge at Ismalia and spot the gray bird on the Arab side—I drive it out of my mind. I never want to be so helpless again.

Constellations of Lifta

1

Lifta is crumbling, it's become
a haven for addicts, prostitutes, vagrants;
they deface the walls with graffiti;
every path in the village is marked with their left-
overs, empty bottles, black plastic bags.

We have to clean them out and
develop a thriving community on this deserted
spot. It's not our place
to save Palestinian heritage, the cost of
preserving these buildings would be astronomical,
in the hundreds of millions of shekels.

2

The houses of Lifta are a haven
for memory; invisible guests come and go
at will in our mosque; the village is home
to the dead in our cemetery, and the unborn
yearn in us to pick figs
from trees our ancestors planted on terraced hillsides.

Now they plan to put up a glittering skyline
to blot out the starting and returning
place of our dreams, the cost to us
would be astronomical: these
traces of our loss
mark the source of our dignity.

On the Front Lines

The incomprehension and hostility of the nations
are nothing new to us. All the arguments
we present in the court of world opinion
are in vain: anyone who isn't living
inside our borders can't grasp the impact
of being totally encircled by enemies.

On the front lines every farmer and bus driver
can hear the difference between a thunder
clap and a missile, and knows it's normal
for a pair of hands to possess ten fingers
that curl around an Uzi in a fight for survival.

After His Likeness

And I thrust my hands into
the land my enemy reddened
with the blood of my brothers

and pulled up a soft wet lump
fertile as shit, and fashioned it
into the image of hatred, after
his likeness. And I carried it

into the field I tilled under the hot
sun and fired it slowly until
it was hard, I took it to bed with me.

And I nestled it against my
chest, it made me feel whole
when fear kept me
from sleeping. Toward dawn

when I drifted off, it suckled
on dreams that mixed the blood-
baths of the past with the latest

incident. The little effigy
grew teeth like a human child,
he took bites out of my flesh
when my nightmares failed

to sate his hunger, he became
mansized over time, the second
self that moved as I moved,

the counterpart I could tell
was always there by the pressure
he put on me in my lying
down and my rising up.

After the massacres, and the wars,
and growing up in the struggle
to live in the same land

as our ancestors, the enemy
and I don't know how to stop
begetting victims and aggressors
for the territories we cohabit.

The World to Come

With the curfew, with the hot sun
at the checkpoint, with the eye my sister
lost to the stone a haredi kid
threw at her in Hebron, with enough
is enough, and the too much
of my father's helplessness churning
in my stomach, and the rubble
of our home at my feet,
they trained me to walk
among them with my vest of dynamite.

With longing for what would come
next—not sleep
stained by the body's sadness
after ecstasy, not the glory
of seeing my face on the walls
of Ramallah, or my mother
stopping many times a day
to visit my photo
in the hallway you go through
every time you enter and leave
the house, not memories
of the horses we rode on the hills
above the refugee camp—
the pressure I lived under
left me no room to become
anything but a bomb.

Now that I've exploded all that
deadness, I'm free
to participate in the rain-
fall and drop into verses
of the sun, thrown
in shimmering dashes and dots
on the ground, and outgrow
bitterness that sprang from
love confined and tortured below,
and develop the spaciousness
of the wind that blows
away the life that murdered me.

III.
ON THE SITE OF LOSS

III
ON THE SITE
OF LOSS

The Coffee House at Lifta

I want to meet you, Yousef,
in the coffee house at Lifta. Let us sit
on the ground and invite History
with a capital H to bow its head and come through
the door in lower case letters. As we speak
of our enemy-uncles, let us make more
room for what we each lost here.

•

I lost my home on this land,
Yoyneh. What did you lose?

•

My uncle Avrom-Yitzkhok
left the narrow alleys where our rebbe rushed by
on slippered feet to tarry with the Impossible
as the Germans were massing on the other side
of the border. Don't cry for me, he told
his mother at the train station, I'm going home.
He became a fighter in the militia
that entered the coffee house and opened fire.
We don't know if he took part
in that raid. He didn't speak of what he did
or didn't do in the war. But this I know:
I've awakened from the dream in which he was my childhood
hero. In the coffee house at Lifta, he nullified the God
my father kept alive in a death camp, and in the DP camp
where I was born, my father wrapped me in his prayer

shawl and carried me into the world of his love
for the Yiddishkeit of our lost shtetl.

•

You ask me to sit down
with you in a place of imaginary
equivalence. There is no door
through which I could meet you there,
only a hole where a door once opened.
Jewish terrorists walked through it
and murdered six of my uncles. No one escaped
without injury. My father carried me
on his back out of Lifta the next morning,
and after two years of wandering
as a beggar, died
of a heart attack, another
victim of the Lifta massacre.

•

There is no hope unless you and I
sit side by side on the site of loss, telling
each other the story of that night.

•

You speak of hope where there is none, if all
you propose is that we mourn together.
And you speak of the story as if it were one
and definitive. You're still living in your own messianic

idea, dreaming
that you can repair your takeover of my homeland
by incorporating me and the Liftawis'
coffee house in a Jewish storytelling ritual.

You would have me sit with you in mud
that was once tiled floor, amid shards
of plaster with traces of pigment
that once were a mural of musicians in a vineyard
under the heavens where a high-vaulted
ceiling sheltered the men who gathered there
to savor time together, sipping
strong black Arab coffee
after their day's labor. And you believe
that if you and I return in memory
to the place where my world came to an end,
we can make our two stories one?

•

Why, then, Yousef, did you welcome
my alliance? Why did you take me
on a guided tour of the ruins?
Why fight to preserve Lifta
as a place of memory?

•

Lest you forget the destruction
your uncle visited on my village. And
as a placeholder for my dead

and my life in parenthesis: this
is where I can bring my past
and future into an encounter with you
and end your erasure of my face.

•

In yeshiva, I learned to draw things toward
the unity in which we sought to live with
God in the world. The template of faith
in which I was taught to think precedes
the new thoughts arising in me, and returns them
to the syntax that formed me. I see, Yousef,
why you reject the terms in which I tried
to communicate my desire. Give me a chance

to try again. I believe that unless
we bring our irreconcilable stories into the same bare
room, unless we sit and listen to each other
mourn the damage
of our mutual history, we will not grow in tolerance
for the other's truth and cease reenacting
the impossibility of peace between our uncles'
warring ghosts. How else
can we be released from our deadlock?

•

No, Yoyneh, the room is not bare, and
the ground on which it stands holds roots
of the fruit-bearing trees we planted and tended
continuously for two thousand years.

You seek reconciliation in the sphere
of the spirit. That will not happen until
there is justice for Palestinians in our own land.
Until you commit yourself to my return
from exile, the situation will remain
what it is—the ruins of possibility.

The Gift

> They thought that after all the suffering
> we had lost our patience.
> —Palestinian folk poem

They see what we hold
in our hands: nothing
but stones.

They break our bones.
And we mend. We practice
dexterity by threading needles.

We hurl outlawed
words at the walls we tag.
They round us up in Suref,
in Nablus, in East Jerusalem.

Wherever they take us, we remain
in the country of our mothers' love.

Two weeks, three weeks, a year—
and we're sitting in the kitchen,
telling the story. Our fathers shake
their fists, our brothers cry
for revenge, our mothers listen
while slicing vegetables and herbs
from the little pockets of garden
they've transplanted from home.

We sip the coffee they spice
with cloves, cardamom
and saffron. We celebrate
the births of our kids,
one by one.

And they see us with nothing—
no country, no occupation
but their Occupation—
nothing to make us men.
We learn how to handle it
from our mothers.
It unsettles them.

They build more settlements
on our hilltops. They keep watch
over our movements. They come for us
past 1 a.m. and slip our heads into burlap
bags, our hands into plastic
cuffs and whisk us to underground
rooms, they interrogate us and we confess.
We have nothing. It's our strongest weapon.

That's not the crime
against their security they want us
to own. They bring in our fathers
and wives dressed in prison garb
and threaten to strip our old men
and spit on their nakedness
and rape our women.

Whatever documents
they set on the table before us,
we sign.

Yes, we advocated shaking
off the Occupation. Yes,
we weren't ignorant of the name
of our activities under their law:
it's terrorism. We are
their terrorists.

After we're released, we get to see
our lawyers. We keep it brief.
What did they do to you?
The usual.
Do you want to file a complaint?
No.

Our compliance isn't sufficient
to allay their anxiety.
Four months, three years, seven years—
in Beit Ummar, in Ramallah, in Tublas,
we're cuffed and hooded.

The procedures they follow aren't,
technically speaking, torture.
The long night of stress
positions resumes. Twenty-two hours of it,
then two hours off. We're returned
to our cells. Small black holes
with a large hole in the middle.

Isolated from changing
light. Forced to lie
in our filth. Not enough space
to lie down or stand up.

We're dying here.
And they are afraid.

They hoist us into the eternal
present of physical pain. Thirty and forty
days of it—high shackling on top
of nonstop shouting and we're hallucinating the end
times. They don't torture us
to extract information. They need us
to populate their security nightmare.

We're dying. And we'll go on
dying—it makes us
terrifying.

They break down
our doors in Nabi Saleh, in 'Ein Beit-al-Ma', in Bureji.
Our kids see us shackled and beaten.
Just as we saw our fathers
beaten.

They still believe
they can crush us. We're forced to extend our arms
and keep them outstretched.
As if their unlimited power over the body
could prove to us the impossibility of holding

the nothing in our hands that they can't shake:
our capacity to wait
and go on waiting beyond the limits of a single lifetime.

In Bethlehem

No faith but the faith
that this can't go on.

They come down from
our hilltops and set
our groves on fire.
They siphon off the Sea
of Galilee and the Jordan
to irrigate the palm
trees in their cities.

No water for three
weeks, then two
days to feel the dignity
of standing in a shower,
washing up, momentarily
eased, the knots
in my body
like beads the water runs
through worried fingers—
how little time I have to fill
my liter bottles against
the next three weeks
of thirst and filth.

None to Accompany Me

Nowhere
in the outcry
on both sides
of Israel/Palestine
is there anyone
who speaks for
me. Alone

among my friends,
I lifted my arms,
dancing *Mayim*
in the fields
I plowed, I harvested
etrogim in Zion.
A girl in love

with a glorious
project, I knew
the happiness of
hard labor in
service to a
utopia. The kibbutz

where I came
of age long ago
was sold off
in the market
for condos. The through-
line of my life
has been severed. Who

doesn't see the shatter-
marks of catastrophe
extending through
the two enemy
populations? My own
grief has no public
face. What

I've lost remains
irreplaceable. Here
in New York, how little
it costs my friends
to repudiate Israel as
an apartheid state.
Amid all their

certitude and clamor,
how can I cry
out for the dream
that is gone
from my life? No one
to mourn with,
no way to make small
steps toward peace.

The Key

the key to the door
that's long gone
hangs from my neck

by day I wait
for the night to return
me to my village

of dreams where I look
for the family
photos I didn't have time to pack

•

of course I took
the key, we expected to come
back in two or three

days, a year later
I walked bent over
from the weight of it

now I don't feel it
around my neck
and then I do

•

innumerable pinpricks
burst through the skin

of my right hand as I
step across the threshold
of the bread shop, my palm
remembers the fluted
doorknob with brass fittings
that I turned every time
I entered our home

•

here the black
hijab makes me invisible, I go
among them, unnoticed
in the crowd of tourists
and black hats, but the young
soldiers circulating through
the alleys of the Old City
eye me cautiously

•

buying butter, I'm
overtaken by the absence
of our butter churn

in the dream
of my village, I go on churning
milk of our goats into butter

but in this shuk
my right arm hangs

from my shoulder
like an empty
sleeve

•

and this citron
is mute, divested
of the orchard where
we used to harvest
it, hands
working in the rhythm
of our song

but then
I pick it up and
remember singing *doves
in our garden
of fruit-bearing trees*

•

the loss keeps its accounts
hidden

sleeps away many of its anniversaries

awakens at an uncertain hour
when it can't help handing over another key
to its pain

which lives on in things I didn't know
I loved

•

thanks to the arrival of fresh
shocks, I remain a daughter
of Lifta, with no capacity
to have armed myself against
a loss made up of untold
losses—how could I
have foreknown what
perishable or overlooked thing
would return to protect
me against the pain
of forgetting

•

I take refuge
in making soup

chopping every-
thing to
bits

hours of handwork

onion days

Going Home

Every step on these hard-
packed dirt streets
hurts. Without money,
without cobblers to work
leather into pliable lasts,
where am I
to find shoes
that take the shape of my footprint?

•

What can I do
with the feet I was
born with? Wide feet
of uneven length. Both
too big and too small
for sneakers that come
in standard sizes.

They blister my toes, they
destroy my arches. Hobbled,
too raw to walk around
for the pleasure of it, I sit
on a crate until boredom
stands me up and undefeated
despair gets me going.

Afoot in my reverie,
I go back over the road
home without leaving

these alleys. Every step
through the refugee camp
burns.

•

Days on end, soaking
my feet in a basin of brackish
runoff, waiting. At night
I hear our horses racing
on our mountaintop
and I take up the journey.

Without shoes
that don't do violence to my flesh,
I set out
for my village where the earth
is molded to the exact measure
of my feet and I ran
as a child barefoot.

•

On barren land, with scant
water, what can I reap
and sow? Here when I trip,
I have the sensation of falling
up, my head seems six feet
aboveground, watching me,
detached from the mishaps
of my feet, I go down

so fast only my body
observes the law of gravity.

IV.
ON THE ROAD
TO JERUSALEM

At the Missing Hearth

> Invent a speech for hope.
> —Mahmoud Darwish, "Counterpoint: For Edward Said"

Let the remnants of my home
be a wound to the landscape
you claim. Let it unsettle you every time
you travel on the road to Jerusalem.

Let it be a face
you can't look at
without hearing a voice
cry, *Don't kill me.*

Let me return
with you to Lifta
and watch your eyes
adjust to the dark inside my house.

Let the abyss
between our two exiles
appear no bigger than the hole
your soldiers blasted through my floor.

You might fall
into my cellar
if you don't move
carefully.

I hope my indignation is
sufficiently tempered by the futility
of the war between us, that I might
imagine this unlikely scene:

Let me invite you
to stand with me at my missing
hearth. Walk across the room
despite your fear that I'll open fire.

First Cousins

You've come to the Land of Israel
late—you're nearly seventy—
what took you so long?

And you think you know something
about us? You crossed the great
distance between your own life

and ours on a direct flight
in a pressure-controlled cabin, without
incident. Here we live moments

away from wailing
sirens; debris and body parts
pile up at our doorstep.

And you come wheeling in your baggage
of opinions, stuffed with unearned
compassion for victims of the Nakba.

You've never held your boyhood
friend in your arms, helpless, watching
his blood run out on the sands of Ashdod.

What is your empathy worth
if it was never tested by destruction?
Why should I give your words weight?

•

Because you know me as a broken
man and a poet, and in the psalms
David sings, The Lord
makes use of broken vessels.

I may not be without bias, but
I have no definite shape, and
before speaking I try to empty myself
of everything I thought I knew,

because I'm receptive to you, and listen
hard, and give your words weight.

•

You won't like what I have to say.
We Jews can't learn to bear reality
in the safe houses of the diaspora.
You're like the evil son at the seder.

You're turning your first trip to Israel
into a pilgrimage to Lifta,
which, sight unseen, you view
as a monument to Palestinian claims.

Every time I pass those ruins by
on the Tel Aviv-Jerusalem highway, I think:
If the war had gone the other
way, that would be us.

But you haven't lived day-to-day
in the history of our people, dreading
the return of the moment when
we'll be blindsided again.

•

Here, you live surrounded by the idea
that the construction of facts
on the ground enhances your security.

But the idea burns up perception
of the real. Israeli land grabs
stoke the fire of retaliatory violence.

Anyone who comes in from the outside
sees metaphors taken as facts, and facts
taken as signs and wonders, and confusion

of metaphor and fact piles up in the word
Zion. The great cubes of stone at Lifta
are shells of Arab homes and metaphors

of a realm of facts that you want to expel
from the hills of Jerusalem
through a monumental real estate project.

•

In Jerusalem, the destruction
of the Second Temple is here and now,

but that Jews come safely from all over
the world to pray at our holiest
ruin will continue only if we go on
fighting for the State of Israel.
Why can't you see that?

•

It seems we are each one-eyed
men in the other's country.

To drink your fill of the Sea of Galilee
you're forced to dissociate the water

that flows through your faucets and irrigates
your front yard from the Occupied Territories.

No matter how far you push them out
of awareness, they return as your security

nightmare: behind your Separation Barrier,
you remain vigilant as you face

the archeology of survival and destruction
that embeds our own day in Biblical time.

•

Aren't you just another
self-hating Jew?

•

The canard ideologues use
to ostracize critics.

•

Would it offend you
if I point out
that I haven't heard much
of the hard
listening you assert
is part of your make-up?

•

Speaking with you
is a trial.
Try me again.

•

When you go to
Lifta, imagine
what that village

would look like
if you also
carried a coffin

on your shoulders
and had to
climb those slopes

stooped.

•

I'd fall
back onto the site
of my own loss,

the ground would
resume its wild
monologue, echoes

of shock
would aggrieve and
numb me.

•

Are you OK? You have this weird
look on your face.

•

When I enter the terrain
where you found refuge, I'm bowed
down by the dead that ride
toward total triumph on my back.

I can't lift my eyes
from every crack in the soil
where I thread my progress
among land mines planted by both sides

in disputed fields. On these green
slopes it's difficult to build modern
houses without shearing off hilltops
and carting the earth away,

and in deserts that don't yield
fruit unless exceptional measures
are taken, I feel the wind
that carried ash of the Shoah

to the Promised Land
and drove new Jews into battle.
You're not alone in hearing
screams of our dying

kin amplified
in the ears of the Jewish
fighters of 1948, deafening them
to any other cry.

Walking with you on streets
named after the kings of ancient Israel
and the authors of the Zionist state,
I can see myself acting as they did.

•

I'm beginning to feel we
are on common ground.

•

I see Ashkenazi boys from the ghettos
of Europe bursting through the door of the coffee house
at Lifta, surrendering to the sensation that pours
from the submachine guns in their arms
through their bodies, in one long wave
of ecstatic violence, washing away a certain phantom
pain, a stinging heaviness, a pressure,
a hollowness in the chest
in which they carried centuries of our exclusion from history,
and one of them is me, I'm there
with them, spraying the room with bullets.

•

You've turned
the key in the door I kept locked
against you, and uttered the one
thing I needed to hear
from you. You identify
with the IDF, the essential Jew
in you flashed up: you
honor Israel's right to exist and defend herself
against all threats to annihilate us.

•

No, my meaning falls in mid-air
out of the words I speak
to you, you erase
my thought, forcing it
into absolute identity with your own idea
or branding it anti-Semitic.

I asked the rabbi with whom I learn Torah,
How is it possible to honor a brutal father,
a crushing mother? *Koved*, he said,
the Hebrew for honor, comes from the root
meaning weight. If you reach beyond
your own trauma and feel the weight of
their lives, you recognize the source
of their actions, and fulfill the commandment.
By following this practice, it's possible for me
to honor the founders of the Zionist state.

As a Jew, I've long identified with the Palestinian
diaspora. Now walking beside you, I
feel you carrying the weight of the eternal Jew-
hatred you believe nothing
can change, and you call this reality;
it fuels the state of war you call Israel.
And I see Lifta is the only gate
through which I could have come to Jerusalem
to face the rage and perplexity of contending with you
and the horror of encountering the murderous tribesman in myself.

Remorse

a van with shaded windows

a photo I stumbled across seventeen years
later

night terrors, over
and over

a gray bird

a litany of place-names

•

a drizzle on the Arava
turned
over the course of two hours into
a hard rain, a flash flood came rolling down the valley
as a single wave

•

the men in the back seat
were hooded

in those days we didn't think
twice about it

•

I thought of it as gray, the bird
dying on the bridge at Ismalia

it wasn't until I'd gone to the Himalayas
and lived among people who'd never heard of Jews
and who lived very well without our Bible and our God,
it wasn't until then

actually it had white speckles
and blue markings

•

I didn't realize the backwards letters
spelled ambulance until I saw one
bearing down on me
in the rear view mirror

•

how the van shook as we rode down
into their villages

Quilaya, Bayt Thul, Bureji, Lifta

past one o'clock, unable to sleep

•

an uncanny resemblance

a lie that provokes tears

a cantorial wind

once upon a time I had a booming
voice

The Messiah

> ...we have been endowed with a *weak* Messianic power, a power to which the past has a claim. That claim cannot be settled cheaply.
> —Walter Benjamin, "Theses on the Philosophy of History"

The False Messiah, in common with His adherents, believed He was the One everyone was waiting for. He was expected eventually to enter Jerusalem, unify the divided city, and bring peace to the Holy Land. Neither He nor those who awaited Him could bear the truth: it was in His nature to exist in a state of infinite deferral.

The messiah, the real one, continually sought to shed his illusions about the world and his place in it. His sole reason for being was to contemplate the earth and arrive at the most complete comprehension that he could bear without being shattered by it. He lived in a state of emergency, sustaining his knowledge and love of mortal life in the face of the wretchedness and horror that, in every era, drove warring parties to submit to the latest iterations of the False Messiah and seek dominion over the Holy Land. The messiah had to endure the violence done to his name and purpose without retaliating. His ultimate task was to see and suffer the impossibility of his coming to the aid of any side in the escalating wars over territory and resources.

In their invincible bias, the contending groups looked for him in the light. His existence would have been an unbroken tedium of isolation and anguish if, in moments of revelation, he didn't behold someone catching sight of him in a beam of shining darkness. He never ceased giving himself to the world in such beams;

they eclipsed what people habitually viewed as reality or immutable law. By abruptly changing their field of vision, he made it possible for their eyes to adjust to the dark, what seemed solid a moment ago dissolved, and they saw their way through their violent fixations—but the False Messiah rarely failed to flood the world with light that made the true way appear impossible.

Nevertheless, the messiah went on saturating the earth with visionary moments. Footfalls of an animal in the crawl space above a synagogue ceiling; a blade of grass, wind- and moon-tipped, a silver wave in a parched field; spooky action at a distance in deep space; changing lines in a patch of sunlight on a prison wall—such occurrences were potential utterances that might make his presence felt by someone singled out to receive it. He spoke all the languages of the world in the sensuous register of shamanic bards or prophets or revolutionaries or physicists or rock stars dreaming of peace; in momentary incarnations, he never ceased arriving.

Little of his surplus of seeing and love came through. Visionary men and women fell into the delusion that they were the ones everyone was waiting for, and did great damage. Of course many persisted in their openness to shocks of messianic disruption. But, whether honored or reviled as proponents of impossible claims, they were denied air time, and suffocated. Even then, a remnant survived, old women and men who went on working against the odds; their reward for being cast into the same nowhere as the messiah was that they were in daily communication with him. After their deaths, a few of these magnanimous and disciplined individuals had streets named after them in cities which continued to be destroyed by man-made hurricanes that behaved like the God of Vengeance. The messiah was gladdened by those who were posthumously recognized as saints or heroes or sublime authors. But his real life—his hope for the world—depended on the hidden ones who transmitted his influence in little deeds to the people among whom they dwelled, who toiled in obscurity, and, in three or four generations, were forgotten.

VISITATION

Amid the wreckage that reached up
to the sky over Gaza, an angel
heard cries that couldn't be
consoled. It hesitated to cross
the horizon that white phosphorus
bombs had turned into a killing field

until it was too late, and the angel,
at the edge of the world, was caught
in the thick of it, eyes
burning, wings
lacerated, unable to breathe
in the shroud of smoke,
in danger of losing sight
of faces blurred in the general air
of destruction, the angel came
down to earth as a poem.

In this poem it visited Ofra who couldn't
be alone in her flat in Maya Hama'avak
after she lost him to friendly fire
in Operation Cast Lead: her son
bowed his head in the corner
above the armoire and showed no
sign he knew she was there. She
wanted to speak to him, but didn't
dare. Lost in his own reverie, he
faded quickly if she so much
as stirred. Hadn't he always been
a light sleeper? She sat still

as a gravestone, and the poem stayed
with her for seven nights, without
disturbing the emptiness in the house
after everyone else was gone.

And the angel, disguised as a page
in an open book, was a friend to
Tibi when his son was gunned down
by a Fatah sniper in a Hamas alley.
He withdrew into his room, banished
the day, his curtains drawn
as the boy at three and twelve and nine
came in and out. Shrieking in delight,
a dice cup in his hands, the boy asked,
What's this? and demanded that he
teach him how to gamble. At seventeen,
solemnly coming home with his first
rifle, taking it apart and hiding the pieces—
he was gone—the boy who had brought
him knees torn where he hit
the ground, crying, *Babba! Babba!
I'm bleeding!* And the poem was
in the dark with the grieving father
like light, adding nothing but itself
to the instants that fled
into the oblivion where the boy was.

Disbelief

And then at dusk, when the white
and yellow Jerusalem stone breathes in the light
and the city softens as if the haze of gold
that rests on all things brought out
the blessed state bestowed by the gaze of the Eternal,
it seems improbable that we cannot live
in peace. The call from the Al-Aqsa Mosque
and the cries from the Wailing Wall
are melodic step-brothers that are sounded
together and ascend as a contrapuntal song.
Does God unravel our prayers
and place them on separate rungs?

Next Year in Jerusalem

1

Lifta was built into
the valley at the western entrance of the city.
Aging villagers drift through,
bearing magnetic ID cards that declare
them present absentees.
From this bowl of ruin, they drink
the life that was, and regain
the power to be wholly present in exile,
drawing gladness and grief from the wadi
at the bottom of the open wound of their history.

Jewish citizens strolling through the last
reserve of green space near the city
want to forget the ghost town that was the site
of a victory in a war long ago settled. Arabs
once lived here. Shadows
flit along the walls and floors
of the exposed interiors of their houses.
They condemn us to see, in the fate
we imposed on them, the image
of ourselves we hate to have mirrored:
this is the open wound of our history.

2

Every year I've concluded
the seder with the inconclusive words Jews everywhere
in the world repeat. Next year when I utter
the prayer that invokes our continuing
exile and redemption of hope,
I will look out at the physical city
from Lifta, and I will see what the last phrase
calls on us to grasp: that even in Jerusalem we are
not in Jerusalem.

Acknowledgements

Thanks to the editors of the following magazines and websites:

The Manhattan Review: "In Jerusalem Stone," "The Return," "Birth Trauma," "The Messiah"

Jewish Currents: "First Cousins"

Tikkun Magazine (www.tikkun.org): "Hinani," "The Coffee House at Lifta," and "Next Year in Jerusalem" are included in my essay, "In the Midst of the Ruins: Activists Struggle to Save the Palestinian Village of Lifta" (Spring 2013 issue)

The Lifta Society Website (previously http://liftasociety.org/news/israel-meets-palestine-a-jewish-poet-encounters-lifta): "Constellations of Lifta," "The Domes of Lifta"

World to Come (an anthology of poems published by *Jewish Currents*: "Disbelief"

The Ruins of Lifta, a film by Menachem Daum and Oren Rudavsky, was the inspiration and a key source of this book. In "Impasse," the statements of the speakers are near-verbatim quotations of Yacoub Odeh and Itzik Shweky, spokespersons for the Palestinian and Israeli positions in the film. The dialogue in "The Coffee House at Lifta" is based on the life-histories and views of Yacoub Odeh and Menachem Daum. For the source of the phrase "undefeated despair" in "Going Home," see John Berger's essay "Undefeated

Despair" in *Hold Everything Dear*. The passage beginning "a drizzle on the Arava..." in "Remorse" is quoted from Jonathan Boyarin's *Palestine and Jewish History*.

Special thanks to Allan Appel, Danny Beagle, Allen Bergson, Riva Danzig, Harriet Fraad, Deena Metzger, Lisa Rubens, Maddy Santner, Mark Weiss, Eileen Wiseman, Steve Zeitlin and Paul Zimet.

IMAGE SOURCES

Cover: Menachem Daum, photographer

Title Page: Menachem Daum, photographer

Pg. vii: Used by permission to FODIP (Forum for Discussion of Israel/Palestine)

Pg. 15: James Emery, "Bethlehem Security Wall and Checkpoint (Israeli side)", used by permission under: https://creativecommons.org/licenses/by/2.0/deed.en

Pg. 27: Artist unknown, detail of a 1948 photograph, the Palestinian exodus, public domain

Pg. 49: Used by permission to FODIP (Forum for Discussion of Israel/Palestine)

A Note about the Author

MARC KAMINSKY is a poet and psychotherapist in private practice in Brooklyn. He is the author of eight previous books of poetry, including *A Cleft in the Rock* (Dos Madres Press), *The Road from Hiroshima* (Simon & Schuster), and *Daily Bread* (University of Illinois Press). His poems, essays and fiction have appeared in many magazines and anthologies, including *The Manhattan Review, The American Scholar, Natural Bridge, The Oxford Book of Aging*, and *Voices within the Ark: The Modern Jewish Poets*. He has published six books on aging, reminiscence and late-life development, and the culture of Yiddishkeit.

Author photo by Madelaine Santner.

OTHER BOOKS BY MARC KAMINSKY
PUBLISHED BY DOS MADRES PRESS

THE CLEFT IN THE ROCK (2018)

FOR THE FULL DOS MADRES PRESS CATALOG:
www.dosmadres.com

Printed by Libri Plureos GmbH in Hamburg, Germany